Spotlight on Social Justice

NATIVE TO THIS LAND

A HISTORY OF INDIGENOUS RIGHTS IN NORTH AMERICA

HEATHER BRUEGL, M.A. (ONEIDA/STOCKBRIDGE-MUNSEE)

TWENTY-FIRST CENTURY BOOKS / MINNEAPOLIS

This is dedicated to the Ancestors who survived so that I could thrive. It is the Ancestors who guide all that I do, and I hope to make them proud. To my family, friends, and husband, all of whom have been my constant rock.

Twenty-First Century Books™
An imprint of Lerner Publishing Group, Inc.
241 First Avenue North
Minneapolis, MN 55401 USA

For reading levels and more information, look up this title at www.lernerbooks.com.

Main body text set in Bembo Std Regular
Typeface provided by Monotype Typography.

Library of Congress Cataloging-in-Publication Data

Names: Bruegl, Heather, author.
Title: Native to this land : a history of Indigenous rights in North America / Heather Bruegl, M.A. (Oneida/Stockbridge-Munsee).
Other titles: History of Indigenous rights in North America
Description: Minneapolis : Twenty-First Century Books, [2026] | Series: Spotlight on social justice | Includes bibliographical references and index. | Audience: Ages 11–18 | Audience: Grades 7–9 | Summary: "Hundreds of Indigenous nations call North America home—and have since before the countries that make up the continent formed. From colonization to modern legislation, learn about Indigenous sovereignty, representation, and rights"—Provided by publisher.
Identifiers: LCCN 2024052974 (print) | LCCN 2024052975 (ebook) | ISBN 9798765644126 (lib. bdg.) | ISBN 9798765684924 (pbk.) | ISBN 9798765682999 (epub)
Subjects: LCSH: Indians of North America—Government relations—Juvenile literature. | Indians of North America—Politics and government—Juvenile literature. | Indians of North America—Legal status, laws, etc.—Juvenile literature. | Indians, Treatment of—North America—Juvenile literature.
Classification: LCC E91 .B78 2026 (print) | LCC E91 (ebook) | DDC 970.004/97—dc23/eng/20250203

LC record available at https://lccn.loc.gov/2024052974
LC ebook record available at https://lccn.loc.gov/2024052975

Manufactured in the United States of America
1 – CG – 7/15/25

CONTENTS

INTRODUCTION

Despite the common misconception that Indigenous people are a thing of the past, hundreds of tribal nations across the US, Canada, and Mexico still call this land home. Some nations in the US are the Lakota, Cherokee, Oneida, Navajo, Ojibwe, and Lenape. In Canada there are the Cree, Métis, and Blackfoot. In Mexico are the Maya, Zapotec, and Nahua, descendants of the Aztecs. And there are many more. Indigenous people are not just a part of history; they are still here, thriving and contributing to their communities.

While reading this book, you will encounter various concepts related to Indigenous people. Self-determination is the ability of Indigenous tribes to control their own government, culture, and resources. Indigenous sovereignty means that Indigenous tribes have the right to govern themselves. They can make laws, protect their traditions, and decide how to run their communities without outside control. Indigenous representation ensures that Indigenous voices and perspectives are included and valued in decision-making processes within Indigenous communities and society. It also includes governments and other institutions acknowledging and respecting Indigenous rights and interests.

The Many Names of Indigenous People

This book will use *Indigenous* when referring to multiple Indigenous groups. But when referring to a specific nation, it will use that group's actual name. Not all nations share one experience, and being specific distinguishes their individual histories. Other terms have also become popular over the years in North America.

- **Indian:** originated with Christopher Columbus when he arrived in the Caribbean. Columbus thought he had made it to the East Indies, so he dubbed all the people he encountered as Indians. Some Indigenous people find the term *Indian* offensive as it is a reminder of colonization and the violence that followed. But other Indigenous people do not have a problem with this word. It is also common in federal policies related to Indigenous peoples and in the official names of many tribes.
- **American Indian:** the people who are native to the land that became the US. The American Indian Movement also uses this term.
- **Native American:** means the same as *American Indian*. This term became the norm in the 1960s and is still widely used.
- **Indigenous:** the original inhabitants of a given land or region
- **Alaska Native:** a member of any of the 229 tribes or nations that are indigenous to Alaska. The terms *Native Alaskan* or *Alaskan Native* may also be used.
- **Inuit:** Indigenous peoples who live in the far north and Arctic areas of Canada
- **Métis:** people who are of mixed Indigenous and European ancestry, primarily from Canada
- **First Nations:** Indigenous peoples in Canada who are not Métis or Inuit
- **Pan-Indian Community:** Indigenous people coming together from different tribes and nations. These groups unite to support shared causes and address common issues such as cultural identity, protecting rights, and advocating for sovereignty.

CHAPTER ONE

Colonization Comes to the "New World"

The year 1492 lives in the minds of Indigenous people as the year that everything changed. When learning about explorer Christopher Columbus in school, students often learn the rhyme, "In 1492, Columbus sailed the ocean blue." But what is usually left out is that Columbus's "discovery" of the New World deeply harmed Indigenous people.

Columbus's Voyage

Columbus planned a three-ship voyage across the Atlantic Ocean to find a new route from Spain to Asia. On October 12, 1492, Columbus and several crew members set foot on an island in the present-day Bahamas, claiming it for Spain. Columbus encountered a group of Indigenous peoples called the Arawak, whom he described as friendly.

Columbus believed that he had reached Asia on his first voyage. After arriving in what is now the Caribbean, he explored Cuba, thinking it was part of mainland China. He also mistakenly identified Hispaniola (now Haiti and the Dominican Republic) as Japan.

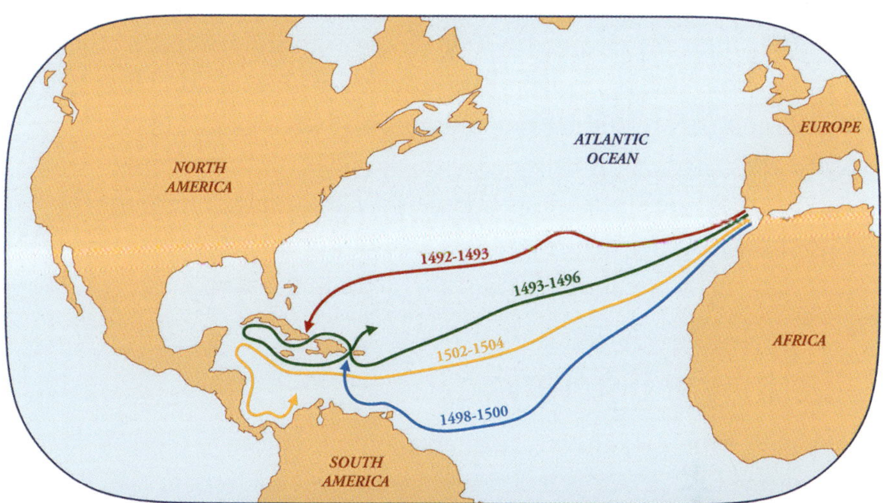

Columbus made four voyages across the Atlantic Ocean, each time landing in regions that Indigenous peoples already inhabited. His arrival led to violent invasions, enslavement, and devastating changes for Indigenous cultures and communities across the Americas.

Forced Labor

Spain celebrated Columbus when he returned from his first trip. On his second voyage, he discovered that the settlement he had left on Hispaniola had been destroyed, and the sailors had been massacred. He thought that the Indigenous population did it, so he established a harsh system of forced labor where Indigenous people had to work for the Spanish settlers. This way Columbus could retain control over the Indigenous population.

> With fifty men, we could subjugate [conquer] them all and make them do whatever we want. Here, there are so many of these slaves.
>
> — Journal of the First Voyage of Columbus

The Spanish also noticed the Natives wore gold jewelry, which shifted their mission to finding wealth. Columbus forced the Indigenous people to help him search for more gold. This exploitation created hatred and tension between the Spanish and the Native populations, with the Spanish threatening violence if the Indigenous people didn't comply. The hunt for gold marked the beginning of a brutal period where many

Doctrine of Discovery

In 1493 Pope Alexander VI issued a statement called the Doctrine of Discovery. It allowed European explorers to claim any land that Christians didn't own. This meant they could take land from the Indigenous peoples living in the regions that later became known as North, Central, and South America. After Columbus voyaged to the Caribbean, the Spanish used the Pope's decree to justify their exploration and colonization of Indigenous lands. Europeans were allowed to take the land and its resources and to force their laws on Indigenous peoples. Indigenous cultures were often destroyed. The doctrine led to displacement, violence, and the erosion of Indigenous rights and sovereignty. It also pushed for converting Indigenous peoples to Christianity.

The Doctrine of Discovery was never officially revoked, but it began losing legal power over time. Still, its influence lasted for centuries. The US Supreme Court referenced it in an 1823 case called *Johnson v. McIntosh* to justify European land claims. While many countries and institutions have moved away from using it, the Vatican only formally denounced it in 2023. It declared that "the church acknowledges that these papal bulls [decrees] did not adequately reflect the equal dignity and rights of Indigenous peoples."

Native lives were lost or harmed because of the European drive for wealth and power.

Colonization in Mexico

North America was home to millions of Indigenous people who ultimately would be forced from their lands. In 1521 a group of Spanish soldiers led by Spanish explorer Hernán Cortés swiftly conquered what is now Mexico just two years after they arrived. The conquest happened quickly because some Indigenous groups, such as the Tlaxcaltecs, allied with Cortés to overthrow the Aztec empire that had been dominating and taxing them. They helped Cortés capture Montezuma, the Aztec leader. In his reports to King Charles V of Spain, Cortés wrote about the great wealth of the Aztec people. After this massive conquest, the Spanish enslaved many Indigenous peoples in Mexico. By 1525 Spain's control extended into Central America. The colonial period in Mexico ended in 1821 when Mexico won its independence from Spain.

Montezuma (*front right*) decided it was wiser to negotiate with Cortés (*left*) in his own city, Tenochtitlan, hoping to form an alliance to protect his empire. He hosted the Spaniards for months, showing them the temples, vast markets, zoos, and palaces of his capital before they imprisoned him.

Indian Boarding Schools in the US and Canada

In both the US and Canada, Indian boarding schools intended to eliminate Indigenous cultures and replace them with European customs and values. Governments and religious organizations established and ran these schools in the late 1800s until the 1970s in the US and until the 1990s in Canada. At these schools, students were not allowed to speak their languages or practice their cultures. They could not wear traditional hairstyles or clothing. Students faced strict rules and discipline, harsh living conditions, and often abuse, which caused a significant disconnect from their heritage. This left lasting scars on individuals and communities, resulting in intergenerational trauma, language loss, and cultural disintegration. Many children returned home after four years or more, unable to connect with their families and communities due to this forced assimilation.

These schools have left lasting effects on Indigenous communities, contributing to ongoing social, economic, and health challenges. This has led to a growing awareness of the need for healing and reconciliation. Efforts are in place to record the stories of survivors, revive languages and cultures, and address the long-term effects of these institutions on Indigenous communities. Canada has taken steps toward reconciliation, such as creating the Truth and Reconciliation Commission in 2008. This commission documents the experiences of boarding school survivors. It also provides ongoing mental health support, financial compensation, and education about the impact of these schools on Indigenous communities. Efforts in both Canada and the US continue to focus on healing, restoring cultures, and recognizing Indigenous rights.

Colonization in Canada

In the 1500s French explorers arrived in northern North America and claimed the land around modern Quebec for the King of France. In 1608 French explorer Samuel de Champlain set up the first permanent French settlement in Quebec. The French wanted the Indigenous people who were already living there to adopt French ways of life and become part of French culture. The French tried to convert them to Catholicism. They also set up the first boarding schools to send Indigenous children to for assimilation.

In the 1670s the British started to explore and claim land in Canada too. They did this by creating a special organization called the Hudson's Bay Company. The company had a Royal Charter, an official document from the British government that allowed it to trade and control land in Canada. The British made policies that took land away from the First Nations people, who had lived there long before the French or British arrived. In 1867 Canada became a self-governing country.

In 1907 at the Swinomish Indian Boarding School in La Conner, Washington, children followed strict routines with tasks such as farming, cooking, and cleaning. Punishments were harsh if they were caught speaking their Native language or practicing any cultural traditions.

CHAPTER TWO

Building a New Nation

The French and Indian War was fought from 1754 to 1763. Great Britain and France sought to dominate the Ohio River Valley and other regions farther north. In 1534 France had claimed an area that later became the province of Quebec. The British had begun colonizing the area in the 1600s, including Quebec, Nova Scotia, Ontario, and the New Brunswick territories. The war was to determine who would have imperial power worldwide. It centered on controlling the rich fur trade and territorial expansion in North America. But this struggle for land ownership excluded the Indigenous tribes that had called this area home for millennia.

French and Indian War

Many Native nations played a role in the war. Many tribes allied with the French because the French had established trading relationships rather than permanent settlements, allowing Indigenous people to maintain control over their lands and continue their own economic practices. The French often married into Native communities and learned Native languages, fostering mutual respect and cooperation. The

After the French and Indian War, Great Britain took the French lands east of the Mississippi, and Spain got the lands to the west. These areas had been home to Indigenous peoples for thousands of years, but their rights were ignored.

Abenaki, Lenape, Ojibwe, Odawa, Shawnee, and Wyandot fought alongside the French.

Unlike the French, British settlers wanted to establish permanent colonies, pushing deeper into Indigenous territories. This expansion often led to the displacement of Native people, the destruction of their lands, and the disruption of their societies. British policies were more focused on dominance and control, which made many Indigenous groups view the British as more aggressive and less trustworthy. However, some Native nations still fought alongside the British. These included the Haudenosaunee, the Cherokee, and the Catawba.

Pontiac's Rebellion and the Proclamation of 1763

The British won the French and Indian War, gaining control over much of North America. The tribes feared that the British would move them west. To prevent this, Pontiac, an Odawa Chief, allied with several other tribes to attempt to drive the British out in 1763. This event became known as Pontiac's Rebellion. The British ended the rebellion but wanted to prevent further conflicts with the tribes. They issued the Proclamation of 1763, which set limits on where British colonists could settle. It stated that colonists could settle anywhere between the Atlantic coast and the Appalachian Mountains and that any land west of the mountains belonged to the Native nations. Many colonists ignored the proclamation and continued to settle in the West despite the rules.

The Stamp, Townshend, and Tea Acts

The British borrowed money to fund the French and Indian War, doubling their debt. British King George III also stationed permanent troops in the American colonies to protect the new territory, mainly from Indigenous resistance, which was costly. He argued that since the war benefited the colonies, American colonists should help pay for it. In 1765 the British Parliament passed the Stamp Act to help pay for the war debt. This was the first tax imposed directly on the American colonies. The Townshend Acts and the Tea Act followed, creating more taxes. Many American colonists felt these taxes were unfair because the American colonies had no representation in the British Parliament. The colonists saw this as taxation without representation, and tensions between the American colonies and Great Britain escalated into war.

REFLECT

How did the French and Indian War impact the creation of the United States? How might Indigenous nations still feel the effects today?

The American Revolution and Native Nations

Tribal nations took different positions during the Revolutionary War (1775–1783). The Mohawk supported the British. The Oneida and Tuscarora sided with the American colonies. The Onondaga favored neutrality.

In 1778 the first Indian treaty in the US was signed with the Lenape people. The treaty allowed the Lenape to send representatives to Congress in return for supporting the colonies against the British during the war. This treaty introduced the idea of Indian representation and recognized the sovereignty of Native nations for the first time. From that point on, the US government used treaties as the primary legal tool in its policies toward Indigenous people.

The Haudenosaunee

After the American Revolution, US leaders took inspiration from Indigenous peoples, the Haudenosaunee (Iroquois Confederacy) in particular, to form a government. The Iroquois Confederacy also influenced the US Constitution by demonstrating principles such as checks and balances and shared power. The original Iroquois Confederacy was called the People of the Longhouse by its members and the Five Nations by white settlers and government officials. The nations that made up the confederacy were the Mohawk, Oneida, Onondaga, Cayuga, Seneca, and later the Tuscarora. The Iroquois Confederacy had made powerful policies for nearly two hundred years. But in 1784 it formally disbanded after the different tribes took different sides during the Revolutionary War.

CHAPTER THREE

Manifest Destiny and the Loss of Land

As settlements across North America grew, settlers needed a way to obtain land from Indigenous people while trying to keep the peace. They used contracts, land agreements, and treaties to remove Indigenous people from their lands and expand westward. Manifest Destiny was the belief that the US was meant to expand to the Pacific Ocean. Many people saw this expansion as inevitable and justified. To achieve this, the federal government enacted various policies.

Indian Removal Act

In 1830 US president Andrew Jackson signed the Indian Removal Act. This act authorized the president to grant unsettled lands west of the Mississippi River to Native Americans in exchange for their lands within existing state borders east of the river. In the Midwest, the Shawnee, Ottawa, Potawatomi, Sauk, and Fox signed treaties and moved to Indian Territory, which later became Oklahoma.

Trail of Tears

In the southeast, the Choctaw, Seminole, Creek, and Chickasaw Nations eventually signed treaties forcing them to move to Indian Territory. But the Cherokee Nation resisted, took its case to the Supreme Court, and won. The Supreme Court decided *Worcester v. Georgia* in 1832, ruling in favor of the Cherokee. This meant that the Indian Removal Act could not be enforced on Cherokee land. But Jackson ignored the Supreme Court's ruling and continued to enforce the Indian Removal Act. By 1838, sixteen thousand Cherokee remained on their land and refused to move. President Martin Van Buren sent in seven thousand US military troops to force the Cherokee to leave.

The Black Hawk War

In 1832 Sauk leader Black Hawk (*pictured*) led the Sauk, Fox, and Kickapoo tribes across the Mississippi River from Iowa Territory to reclaim their ancestral lands in Illinois. They had felt forced to sign the treaties that gave away their land. They saw the US government's broken promises and the arrival of settlers as a betrayal.

The US government saw Black Hawk's return as a treaty violation. This sparked the Black Hawk War (April–August 1832). After five months, US forces defeated Black Hawk at the Battle of Big Axe and imprisoned him and other leaders for a year. Upon release from prison, Black Hawk returned to Iowa Territory.

The US government forced the Cherokee and other tribal nations to walk to Indian Territory. This became known as the Trail of Tears. Along the way, almost ten thousand Indigenous people died of disease, cold, and hunger. By the 1840s a total of fifty thousand Indigenous people were moved off their lands during westward expansion, opening 25 million acres (10.1 million ha) of land to white settlers.

REFLECT

How do you think the experience of walking hundreds of miles during the Trail of Tears impacted Indigenous communities physically, emotionally, and culturally?

The Dawes Act

Henry Dawes was a US senator and the chairman of the Committee on Indian Affairs. Dawes believed that by dividing tribal lands and giving individual plots to Indigenous people, they would assimilate into white American society. In 1887 the General Allotment Act, or Dawes Act, became law.

Before the Dawes Act, all members of a tribe communally owned reservation land. The Dawes Act divided communal land into individual allotments. To receive a land allotment, Indigenous people had to be registered on base rolls. This began the practice of using base rolls to determine tribal membership. These older base rolls are still used to determine tribal citizenship in modern times.

The Dawes Act also encouraged Indigenous people to farm and wear white people's clothing in the hope that this would lead them to abandon their "Indian ways." But much of the land given to Indigenous people in Indian Territory was dry, rocky, and unsuitable for farming. In addition, many Indigenous people didn't want to take up farming because it wasn't their traditional way of life.

The Dawes Act was presented as a way to protect Indigenous land rights through individual allotments. Instead, it undermined communal land ownership and harmed Indigenous cultures. It ultimately benefited US interests by opening remaining lands to settlers, contradicting its supposed aim of protecting Indigenous land rights.

Lone Wolf v. Hitchcock

The significant court case *Lone Wolf v. Hitchcock* emerged from the Dawes Act. Kiowa chief Lone Wolf the Younger, speaking for the Kiowa, Comanche, and Apache tribes, argued that Congress broke the Medicine Lodge Treaty of 1867. The treaty required approval from at least three-fourths of the men living on the reservation before any changes could be made to their land. This rule aimed to protect their land from being taken or altered without their approval.

Even though the Supreme Court ruled against Lone Wolf the Younger, he remained an advocate for Kiowa land rights and cultural preservation.

In 1892 Congress opened 2,000,000 acres (809,371 ha) of their land to settlers without their permission. The US Supreme Court ruled that Congress could take reservation land without approval because of the Dawes Act. The Supreme Court also ruled that Congress could void treaty obligations because it had inherent absolute power. For the first time, it was officially declared that the US government had no obligation to protect the rights of Indigenous people.

CHAPTER FOUR
The Union Breaks

By 1860 the US was on the brink of civil war. The war was fought largely over enslavement. The North argued that enslavement was immoral and should be outlawed, and the South argued that it was a states' rights issue and the backbone of their economy.

Many tribal nations fought in the Civil War (1861–1865), including the Lenape, Creek, Cherokee, Osage, Shawnee, Pequot, Odawa, and Huron. Like many families divided between the North and the South, some tribes had members fighting on both sides. And some battles of the Civil War occurred in Indian Territory.

The Cherokee and the Civil War

Before their removal to the Indian Territory, the Cherokee had lived in areas of modern North Carolina, Tennessee, and Georgia. In hopes of stopping the government from removing them from their land, the Cherokee had "civilized" themselves by writing down their language, starting a newspaper, building schools, and in some cases, running prosperous plantations and enslaving people to work on them.

At the start of the Civil War, the Cherokee Nation was divided on whether to remain neutral or support the Southern Confederacy. The Cherokee Nation came to a consensus in 1861 and allied with the Confederacy. In 1862 Stand Watie was elected chief of the newly declared Southern Cherokee Nation in Indian Territory. He pledged Cherokee support to the Confederate cause. Watie eventually became a general in the Confederate Army.

General Watie was the last Confederate general to surrender during the Civil War.

Cherokee leaders signed a treaty transferring all the promises made to the Cherokee by the US federal government to the Confederate States. This treaty promised to protect the Cherokee people, their livestock, food rations, and other goods. The Cherokee were required to offer ten companies of soldiers and allow military construction on Cherokee land.

The Civil War negatively impacted the Cherokee Nation more than any other tribe. Their population declined from twenty-one thousand to fifteen thousand due to wartime deaths. While the US government promised to pardon all those involved in the Confederacy after the South was defeated, this did not apply to the Cherokee. The US government saw the entire Cherokee Nation as disloyal and revoked many of their rights, including their land rights.

The Treaty of 1866

In 1866 the US government imposed a new treaty on the Cherokee, forcing them to give up large portions of their land in Indian Territory. The Treaty of 1866 stated that they also had to free any enslaved people they held and grant them and their descendants citizenship within the Cherokee Nation. The US government gave these former enslaved individuals, known as Freedmen, 160 acres (65 ha) of land in Indian Territory for each household. The treaty also stated that the Freedmen would have voting rights within the Cherokee Nation. The Cherokee updated their constitution to include the Freedmen, but some people resisted. Many Cherokee people struggled to accept the Freedmen as full members of the nation, feeling that the federal government had forced

In 2011 Freedmen descendants protested outside of the Bureau of Indian Affairs (BIA) in Muskogee, Oklahoma, to defend their Cherokee tribal membership. In 2021 the Cherokee Nation resolved the issue by guaranteeing Freedmen equal citizenship rights in its new constitution.

this change. Segregation between the Cherokee and Freedmen occurred within the nation, mirroring wider American society.

The Dakota Uprising

Around the time of the Civil War, another conflict in the Midwest affected tribal nations. Confronted with increasing white settlement, the Dakota signed a treaty called the Treaty of Traverse de Sioux in 1851, which promised annuity payments. These annual payments by the US government were supposed to help the Dakota recover after ceding their land during westward expansion. However, the payments were delayed, and food supplies ran low, putting the Dakota at risk of starvation.

In 1858 when Minnesota became a state, several Dakota bands led by Little Crow traveled to Washington, DC, to demand that the US government honor its treaties, including the Treaty of Traverse de Sioux. The government dismissed their demands. Later, when the Dakota asked for food, payment, and supplies, officials in Minnesota refused. Little Crow said, "We have waited a long time. The money is ours, but we cannot get it. We have no food, but here these stores are filled with food. We ask that you, the agent, make some arrangement by which we can get food from the stores, or else we may take our own way to keep ourselves from starving." At another meeting, the Dakota asked if they could buy food on credit. Trader Andrew Jackson Myrick responded, "If they are hungry, let them eat grass or their own dung."

In August 1862 a Dakota hunting party stole eggs from farmers in Acton Township, which led to the deaths of five settlers. Chief Little Crow held a War Council. The council decided to continue attacking in hopes of receiving the

Taoyateduta (Little Crow)

Taoyateduta, meaning His Scarlet Nation, also known as Little Crow, grew up near the Mdewakanton village of Kaposia. Some white settlers lived in Kaposia after the Mdewakanton were forced to move from the area. This gave Little Crow insight into European ways of life and how the US government operated. He was a negotiator and signed the Treaty of Mendota in 1851 and the Treaty of 1858. He described to his people what was happening to tribes in the eastern US:

> "We are only little herds of buffaloes left scattered; the great herds that once covered the prairies are no more. See!—the white men are like the locusts when they fly so thick that the whole sky is a snowstorm. . . . Count your fingers all day long and white men with guns in their hands will come faster than you can count."

He used his understanding of European culture to lead the Dakota Uprising in 1862. After the uprising, Little Crow fled to Canada to gather continued support. Shortly after he returned to Minnesota, he was killed while picking raspberries with his son, Wowinape, in 1863.

Little Crow combined traditional Dakota values with careful planning, encouraging unity among tribes and strengthening their political and military power.

In 1862 the US military hanged thirty-eight Dakota whom Lincoln singled out, with one being spared at the last minute. About four thousand people showed up to watch the execution in Mankato, Minnesota.

promised payments and driving out the settlers from Dakota lands. Little Crow led a raid against the Lower Sioux Agency, where Myrick was killed and grass stuffed in his mouth. The Dakota then attacked the towns of New Ulm and Fort Ridgely. Nine days later, fourteen hundred armed US soldiers arrived, and the Dakota realized they could not win. By September, Little Crow retreated.

After the Dakota surrendered, the US military trials began. US courts sentenced more than three hundred Dakota to death. Defendants didn't have legal counsel, and each trial lasted about five minutes. President Abraham Lincoln approved the execution of thirty-nine Dakota who were convicted of crimes against civilians.

REFLECT

How do you think the Civil War and the Dakota Uprising impacted the long-term relationship between Indigenous nations and the US government?

CHAPTER FIVE

Reorganization and Tribal Membership

During the Great Depression (1929–1941), Indian Country, which included the self-governing tribal nations across the US, suffered even more than non-Native groups. But some change was coming. Sociologist and activist John Collier believed that Native cultures were at risk due to forced assimilation into white society. He had formed the American Indian Defense Association in 1922 to fight for Indigenous rights and would do more after the Great Depression began.

Indian Reorganization Act

In 1933 President Franklin D. Roosevelt appointed John Collier as Commissioner of Indian Affairs. In 1934 Collier introduced the Indian Reorganization Act (IRA) to reverse some of the harm caused by the Dawes Act. The IRA ended the allotment policy and banned the future sale of Indigenous lands. It returned unallotted lands to tribes, except for land already purchased by non-Native people. The government could also buy back land from non-Native people and place it under tribal trust status. By putting land into trust status,

In 1934 Blackfoot chiefs met with Collier (*third from left*) in South Dakota to discuss the IRA.

the US government holds the land title for the direct benefit of the tribes, which helps protect the land from being sold or developed without tribal approval.

The IRA also granted tribal communities some governmental and judicial independence, provided they adopted a structure similar to the US system, which had already been modeled after the Haudenosaunee. While the IRA referred to tribes as autonomous communities that could govern themselves, it also treated them as wards of the federal government, meaning the government retained some control over them. Traditional Indigenous leaders questioned the act and saw it as another mandate to live in white institutions. Other Indigenous people had mixed reactions to the IRA. Some praised Collier, while others criticized him, saying he did not recognize the diversity of Native lifestyles.

Blood Quantum

The IRA also introduced the idea of blood quantum and how to define what it meant to be "Indian." Blood quantum is a system created by the federal government to determine tribal citizenship and who is considered Indigenous. People use it to measure how much Indigenous ancestry someone has, usually shown as a percentage. They calculate this percentage using tribal and ancestry documents, with the original member of a tribe considered 100 percent Indigenous based on official census records. For example, if one parent is full-blooded Indigenous from a specific tribe and the other parent has no Native blood, their child would be considered to have a blood quantum of one-half, or 50 percent.

Government officials hoped that if enough Indigenous people intermarried, fewer people would be seen as Indigenous over time. Officials believed that if there were fewer people who could legally be part of a tribe, treaties would become null and void. This would allow the government to ignore the agreements they made to protect Indigenous lands and rights.

Blood quantum was not something that tribes had previously used, so there wasn't anyone in the tribes keeping track of it when the IRA was implemented. Citizenship or membership in a tribal nation was fluid and organic. However, government agents had started creating base rolls and estimating people's blood quantum in the late 1800s under the Dawes Act. Other times, the government brought in anthropologists. They used hair texture, the shape of the nose and eyes, skin color, and foot width to determine how "Indian" someone was. But many Indigenous people were distrustful of the government and were never counted. That meant they never ended up on the base rolls, thus making their descendants unable to enroll to receive the benefits from the IRA. This issue still exists in modern times.

Tribal Nations and Blood Quantum

The idea of blood quantum has become a way of life for Indigenous people. Blood quantum is still used to help determine who is eligible for citizenship in a tribal nation. Each tribal nation has its own requirement for a blood quantum. Some nations require a minimum blood degree for members born outside of reservation boundaries. The ability of tribal nations to determine who is and isn't a member is considered an essential element that gives the tribes their sovereignty.

Defining the Word *Indian*

The IRA also attempted to define the term *Indian*. Collier proposed that the definition of *Indian* include tribal members, their descendants who resided on reservations, and those with at least one-fourth Indian blood. Several members of Congress, including Montana senator Burton Wheeler, saw this definition as too broad and objected to it:

> "I do not think the government of the US should go out here and take a lot of Indians in that are quarter bloods and take them in under the provisions of this act. . . . What we are trying to do is get rid of the Indian problem rather than to add to it."

Wheeler also said that all people who were less than half Indian should not be able to receive IRA benefits because they were basically "white people." As a result of the objections, when Congress passed the IRA, they used Collier's definition of Indian but raised the threshold to half-blood.

Membership, descent, residence, and blood components were specific methods for defining what it meant to be Indian. The half-blood and descendant categories expanded the federal definition of *Indian* beyond tribal membership. But the definition required some Indian blood, no matter what. This excluded people with no Indian ancestry who were married into or adopted by the tribe. Overall, the IRA aimed to empower tribes but created confusion regarding membership and eligibility for federal benefits.

REFLECT

Do you think the Indian Reorganization Act strengthened tribal sovereignty? Why or why not?

Tribal Membership in Canada and Mexico

Canada also has a system that allows Indigenous people to enroll as First Nations people. It is called Indian status and is managed by the federal government. This law was first passed in 1876 and has changed over time. This registration grants Indigenous people legal recognition and access to certain rights, benefits, and protections from the government, such as health care, education, and housing on reserves.

In Mexico there is a large Indigenous population, but the government does not have a system where people can officially join or be enrolled in a specific tribe. While Mexico recognizes Indigenous people, it does not recognize tribal nations. It views Indigenous people as a single group within the broader Mexican population. The government recognizes Indigenous people's cultural and linguistic diversity but does not manage or monitor membership like the US or Canada do.

CHAPTER SIX

Citizenship and Civil Rights

It seems logical to assume that since Indigenous people have been in North America for thousands of generations, they would automatically be made citizens when the US was created. However, that is not what happened. Indigenous people were in a strange and unique position under federal law because they were not fully recognized as citizens.

Indigenous people could receive US citizenship in a few ways. Indigenous women could be granted citizenship if they married a non-Indigenous white man, but that sometimes meant giving up their tribal citizenship and any rights to tribal land. Indigenous people could be granted citizenship if they served in the military, but this wasn't guaranteed.

During World War I (1914–1918), about twelve thousand Indigenous people served in the military. They faced unfair and discriminatory treatment during and after service. Indigenous military veterans were not entitled to the same benefits as others who had served because they were not citizens. This highlighted the need for a more inclusive and clearer policy for citizenship. After World War I, there was a massive push to make Indigenous people US citizens.

Indian Citizenship Act

The US government passed the Indian Citizenship Act in 1924. The law's main goal was to ensure that Indigenous people, including veterans, would receive the same rights and benefits as US citizens. To do so, it granted US citizenship to all Indigenous people born in the United States.

Some traditional Indigenous leaders saw the act as a way to integrate Indigenous people into mainstream American culture, which they didn't approve of doing. The act also reflected the ongoing challenges and tensions related to Indigenous sovereignty and self-determination. The IRA of 1934 aimed to strengthen tribal self-governance and preserve Indigenous cultures, responding to the limitations of the Indian Citizenship Act. Together, these two laws highlighted the ongoing struggle for Indigenous people to balance their identities as citizens with their rights as members of sovereign nations.

Four Osage leaders met with US president Calvin Coolidge (*center*) after he signed the bill granting Indigenous people citizenship in 1924.

Voting Rights

While the Indian Citizenship Act granted US citizenship to Indigenous people, it did not automatically grant voting rights. State governments decided whether Indigenous people had the right to vote.

In 1938, seven US states refused to grant suffrage to Indigenous people. New Mexico was among the last states to

Granting Citizenship in Canada and Mexico

Canada did not grant citizenship to its First Nations people until 1947, and their rights grew over several years. In 1956 the Canadian Citizenship Act was amended to grant citizenship to First Nations and Inuit people who entered Canada before 1947. In 1960 First Nations people received the right to vote in Canadian federal elections. In 1982 the Canadian government officially recognized the voting rights of First Nations people in its constitution. With all these legal protections, First Nations people gained better access to voting and participation in government.

In 1824 Mexico's constitution granted Indigenous people the right to vote and to hold public office, but these rights were often ignored. During the colonial period, Spanish colonizers enslaved Indigenous people and exploited them as laborers, leading to a long history of discrimination and dehumanization that continues to impact their lives in modern times. In 2001 the Mexican government passed a constitutional reform that recognized the rights of all Indigenous people, which included improving access to voting. This reform finally ensured Indigenous voices and cultures were acknowledged and respected in Mexico's democracy.

Members of the Hiawatha First Nations cast their ballots for the first time in 1960.

extend voting rights to Indigenous people, doing so in 1962. However, like other marginalized racial and ethnic groups in the US, Indigenous people wouldn't be able to vote freely until the passage of the Voting Rights Act of 1965, which prohibited racial discrimination in voting.

The Termination Era

In 1953 the US federal government officially adopted a termination policy. Termination aimed to end the legal status of Indigenous nations, dissolve tribal governments, stop federal recognition of tribes, and open tribal land for sale to non-Indigenous people. The policy made every Indigenous person within the territorial US subject to the same laws, privileges, and responsibilities as everyone else. It also severed treaty responsibility and obligations on the federal government's side. Termination made it even harder for tribes to keep their identities, adding to the already significant losses of language, culture, and ceremony.

Between 1953 and 1964, the US government stopped recognizing 109 tribes. It took away tribal nations' control of their land, and control over legal matters moved from tribes to state governments. The government took 3 million acres (1.2 million ha) of land, and twelve thousand Indigenous people lost their tribal status. The government sold that land to non-Natives, removed federal services and protections, and caused reservations to disappear. Many tribes tried to fight termination, but with limited funds and poor conditions, they couldn't succeed.

Indian Relocation Act

Congress passed the Indian Relocation Act during the Termination Era. This 1956 act encouraged Indigenous

Graduates from the BIA relocation and work program leave for jobs in Los Angeles, California, in 1956. By 1960 more than thirty-one thousand Indigenous people moved to urban cities from their reservations.

people throughout the US to leave reservations, move to urban areas to find jobs, and assimilate into "mainstream" society. The government offered assistance including job training, education, and help with moving. The concept of relocation had first begun in 1951, when the BIA created a relocation and work program. This program encouraged Indigenous people living on tribal land in Oklahoma, New Mexico, California, Arizona, Utah, and Colorado to move to more urban areas. The following year, they extended the program to all Indigenous people.

When Indigenous people moved to cities, they often felt isolated from their communities. They faced racial and job discrimination and segregation. There was also no guarantee of finding work, so many faced unemployment. But some

Indigenous people who relocated to urban areas formed pan-Indian communities. They began to work together and organize to achieve rights such as self-determination, civil rights, and sovereignty.

Indian Civil Rights Act

After receiving US citizenship in 1924, Indigenous people still faced unique challenges regarding which rights applied to them. In 1896 the US Supreme Court had ruled in *Talton v. Mayes* that the Fifth Amendment to the US Constitution did not apply to Indigenous people or tribal governments. The Fifth Amendment protects individuals from self-incrimination, guarantees the right to a grand jury, and forbids double jeopardy. Double jeopardy means a person cannot be tried twice for the same crime once found innocent or guilty. The Fifth Amendment also has the Just Compensation clause. It means that if the government takes land, it must pay the owner a fair amount for it. Despite receiving citizenship in 1924, Indigenous people still did not have the protections of the Fifth Amendment in US courts.

Congress passed the Indian Civil Rights Act in 1968. Under it, Indigenous tribes gained some protections from the Fifth Amendment but not all. The act guaranteed that in tribal courts, Indigenous people had the right to know what they were being accused of and the right to a fair trial. The tribal courts couldn't take away their life, liberty, or property without following legal procedures per the US Constitution. But tribal courts were still not required to provide free lawyers for people who couldn't afford them, and there wasn't a right to a jury trial in every situation. Since tribes had their own governments, they didn't have to follow every rule that the US government did.

Self-Determination and Education Assistance Act

By the 1960s, Indigenous nations were focused on fighting for their sovereignty. Because of the continued work of activists, Congress passed the Self-Determination and Education Assistance Act of 1975. One of the first things the act did was officially end the termination policy. The act allowed Indigenous tribes to take back control of services such as health care and housing that the federal government previously ran. It also gave tribal nations control of tribal schools, and teachers reintroduced Native languages to students. And tribes regained tribal governments, which led to the revamping of tribal courts. The act also created new business and job opportunities on reservations. The act as a whole empowered tribal governments to make decisions that better reflected the needs of their communities, marking a significant step toward the restoration of tribal sovereignty.

The Hupa Indian K'ima:w Medical Center, located on the Hoopa Valley Indian Reservation in California, is known for addressing the unique needs of the Hupa and other Indigenous peoples in the area, blending modern medical practices with respect for traditional healing methods.

REFLECT

How do you think having control over education and health care impacts a tribe's ability to preserve its culture and traditions?

CHAPTER SEVEN

The American Indian Movement

By the late 1960s the Civil Rights Movement was in full force. From Black rights and the fight for racial equality to the struggle for LGBTQ+ rights, many groups demanded fundamental human and civil rights. Indigenous people were no different in their fight for civil rights and sovereignty. Protests broke out nationwide as people pushed for fair treatment and change. During this time, the American Indian Movement (AIM) took action to address the specific challenges Indigenous communities faced and to defend their rights.

Seated, left to right: **AIM founders Clyde Bellecourt and Dennis Banks met with Senator Walter Mondale in 1971.**

Native American activists Dennis Banks and Clyde Bellecourt formed AIM in 1968 in Minneapolis, Minnesota. It addressed issues within Indian Country, such as sovereignty, treaty rights, poverty, education, racism, and police brutality. AIM activists organized mass protests nationwide and used media to raise awareness of Indigenous rights and issues.

AIM Founders

Dennis Banks was from Minnesota and went to an Indian boarding school. When he was nineteen, he joined the air force but struggled with alcoholism and crime. In 1966 he went to prison, where he met Clyde Bellecourt. Bellecourt was born on the White Earth Reservation in Minnesota. Both Banks and Bellecourt were Indian boarding school survivors.

Several women in the movement were also essential to the success of AIM. They include Madonna Thunder Hawk, Phyllis Young, Lorelei DeCora Means, and Janet McCloud. In 1974 they founded Women of All Red Nations (WARN). The group, which is still active, was established independently of AIM to specifically address the unique challenges faced by Indigenous women.

Besides being a part of AIM and WARN, Madonna Thunder Hawk is one of the cofounders of the Warrior Women Project with her daughter Marcella Gilbert.

Alcatraz Protest

Alcatraz Island, located near San Francisco, California, started as a fort in the 1850s and then became a federal prison in 1861. Over the years, it became infamous for holding dangerous criminals such as Al Capone and George "Machine Gun" Kelly. When the prison closed in 1963, Indigenous people in the San Francisco Bay area began pushing to turn the island into a cultural center and school. In 1969 a fire burned down San Francisco's American Indian Center. A group called Indians of All Tribes turned to the unused land of Alcatraz Island and organized an occupation. Activist and Mohawk tribal member Richard Oakes led the occupation, saying, "If a one-day occupation by white men on Indian land years ago established squatter's rights, then a one-day occupation of Alcatraz should establish Indian rights to the island."

Activists added graffiti around Alcatraz Island with sayings such as "Red Power" and "Custer had it coming." There was a sign painted on the water tower that read, "Peace and Freedom. Welcome."

On November 20, under the cover of night, eighty-nine Native Americans including many AIM activists sailed to Alcatraz Island and claimed it for all tribes. They demanded that the federal government provide funds to create an Indigenous university and cultural center. The Richard Nixon Administration left the protesters alone since they remained peaceful. However, other government officials went to the island several times to negotiate an end to the occupation. By the beginning of 1970, the dynamic on the island had changed. Many activists were students who had to leave the island to return to school. Then, citing the need to fix a lighthouse and a foghorn, heavily armed federal forces ended the occupation of Alcatraz on June 11, 1971. While the protest ended without much changing, it fueled Indigenous activists to organize other smaller protests and occupations across the country, including protests at Plymouth Rock and Mount Rushmore.

Trail of Broken Treaties Protest

In 1972 a cross-country protest brought awareness to broken treaties, inadequate housing, and low living standards in Indigenous communities. This protest was called the Trail of Broken Treaties. The caravan, organized by AIM, started on the West Coast in October, with more than seven hundred protesters reaching Washington, DC, in November, one week before the presidential election. Government officials canceled meetings with protesters due to concerns about potential unrest and disruptions so close to the presidential election, and President Nixon was out of town. The protesters became increasingly frustrated. They occupied the BIA offices to make their demands heard. The Nixon Administration at first refused to meet with the protesters or receive the twenty-point paper that defined their demands, such as being involved in treaty negotiations, honoring current treaties, and returning land. After a week, the protest ended with talks by AIM members and Nixon Administration officials, who promised to include Indigenous communities in future treaty negotiations.

Wounded Knee Massacre

The first conflict at the Wounded Knee settlement on the Pine Ridge Reservation in South Dakota occurred in December 1890. It began with the revival of the Ghost Dance movement, a ceremony that promised a return to Indigenous peace and prosperity. Tavibo, a northern Paiute prophet, originally led the Ghost Dance in 1870. He spoke of a future where Indigenous people would live in peace and harmony again because the white people would return to Europe. The movement died down when the prophecy did not come true. But in 1889, Wovoka, a northern Paiute spiritual leader, revived the movement. Wovoka's vision offered hope that the land, buffalo, and ancestors would return, restoring life from before colonization. The Lakota and other Plains nations embraced the dance, hoping it would help them resist further loss of their lands.

However, white settlers saw the Ghost Dance as a threat. The US government outlawed it, fearing it was a call to war. Chief Sitting Bull, a respected Lakota leader and supporter of the Ghost Dance, was arrested due to fears he might inspire resistance. During his arrest, he was killed by police. Chief Big Foot (Spotted Elk) led 350 Lakota to seek safety at Pine Ridge Reservation.

Wounded Knee Occupation

In 1973 the tribal government on the Pine Ridge Reservation struggled with corruption. This reservation is where the well-known Wounded Knee Massacre occurred in 1890. The tribal chairman, Dick Wilson, was corrupt. He relied on his security forces, known as the Guardians of the Oglala

Indigenous people participating in a ritual Ghost Dance in 1890. Participants often wore special shirts and dresses decorated with symbols of nature, the elements, and feminine power to serve as a form of protection, connection with ancestors, and assertion of cultural identity.

The Seventh US Cavalry surrounded the group of Lakota and started to disarm them. A deaf Lakota man tried to explain that he had paid a lot for his rifle, and it was accidentally fired. In response, soldiers shot into the crowd of Native Americans who had tried to run. Soldiers murdered between 250 and 300 Native Americans, most of whom were women and children. This event became known as the Wounded Knee Massacre.

Nation, to maintain control. Wilson's administration used intimidation and violence against his political opponents and others who challenged his authority. Many people who spoke up against him ended up dead. This environment of fear and corruption deeply affected the community.

AIM had become known for taking strong stances on Indigenous rights, and traditional Oglala Lakota members on Pine Ridge highly respected the movement. The elders invited AIM members to stand on the sacred ground of Wounded Knee, believing their presence could rally support for reform and protect the community from Wilson's oppressive tactics. AIM agreed to support them. By standing on the sacred ground, AIM and local leaders sent a powerful message that the historical injustices against Indigenous people were ongoing and demanded action. The occupation wasn't just about Wilson. It became a larger protest about broken treaties, injustice, and the right to self-governance.

Elder Frank Fools Crow, one of the leaders at the Wounded Knee occupation, traveled to the United Nations (UN) for recognition of the Oglala Nation, but the nation, while asserting sovereignty, didn't meet the criteria of a recognized state. The UN recognizes states with established governments, clear borders, and international diplomatic relations.

The AIM protesters had several demands, including removing Wilson from office. They also wanted a revival of treaty talks with the federal government. They set up barricades to block people from entering the town, and gunfire erupted each night. During the occupation, the protesters at Wounded Knee declared themselves the independent Oglala Nation and demanded to speak with the US secretary of state. They did not succeed in meeting with the secretary of state, and the occupation ended after seventy-one days when both sides agreed to disarm following negotiations. The US government arrested many of the protesters, and tensions in the area remained high.

The Wounded Knee occupation raised national and international awareness about the issues facing Indigenous communities in the US, highlighting the struggles for sovereignty, justice, and treaty rights. This occupation drew widespread media attention, revealing to the public the depth of Indigenous grievances, including government neglect, broken treaties, and issues of corruption within tribal governments supported by federal agencies.

Assembly of First Nations

While AIM worked to fight for the rights of Native Americans in the US, the Assembly of First Nations (AFN) advocated for First Nations people in Canada. The AFN formed in 1982. After years of fighting for self-government in the 1970s, First Nations leaders realized they needed a way to respond directly to government policies that affected them. The AFN represents around nine hundred thousand First Nations people in Canada. The group works on important issues such as land treaties, Indigenous rights, and environmental resources. It meets twice a year, and a Council of Elders helps set the rules and procedures for the group.

REFLECT

AIM's work continues. How do you think AIM impacts modern Indigenous communities and their fight for rights?

CHAPTER EIGHT

We Are Still Here

Indigenous people have continued to confront systemic injustices and advocate for their rights. Three crucial aspects of this ongoing struggle for justice are the Indian Child Welfare Act (ICWA), which seeks to protect Indigenous children and uphold the rights of families and tribes in the face of discriminatory practices; efforts to reclaim land; and increased representation in government.

Indian Child Welfare Act

The US government used a powerful method to break Indigenous people—taking their children. First the government forced Indigenous children into boarding schools to erase their culture. Then it stole Native children and adopted them into non-Native families. The Indian Adoption Project began in 1958 as a collaboration between the BIA and the Child Welfare League of America. The goal was to force Indigenous children to assimilate.

Social workers, often working for government agencies or religious organizations, assessed Indigenous families to decide which children should be removed. Many children were taken from their families without consent, often under the assumption that their home environments were unsuitable. In some cases, children were taken directly from school without parental knowledge, which left families confused and unaware of their children's whereabouts. Families were not provided with clear or truthful information about the reasons behind these removals. Indigenous families started reporting their children missing. In response, Congress passed the ICWA in 1978 to protect Native children.

Congress identified three reasons for the high number of Native children being removed from their families. First, non-Native social workers didn't understand Indigenous culture and didn't attempt to notify parents and family members about adopting out their children. Second, living conditions in Indigenous communities were poor, and reservations were underfunded. From the outside, reservations didn't seem like safe places to live, even though a strong sense of community surrounded the children. Third, the BIA was paying social workers to take children from their homes.

The ICWA aimed to keep Native children within their communities and protect their rights to their culture and family connections. The ICWA made sure that states could not control adoption or custody hearings for Native children living on reservations. Instead, the law gave control to tribal governments, allowing them to create their own rules for child welfare cases. This meant that tribal courts handled these matters, prioritizing tribal customs and the child's best interests as determined by the tribe. Because of the protections ICWA provides, it is still the highest standard for ensuring Native children are placed in Native homes when they are adopted or placed in foster homes.

In 2022 hundreds of people protested outside the US Supreme Court while it heard arguments about the ICWA. In 2023 the court upheld the ICWA in *Haaland v. Brackeen*, confirming that Native children should be placed with Native families whenever possible and efforts must be made to keep Native families together.

The ICWA also highlights the unique relationship between tribal nations and the US. The US government does not classify Native people by race but as members of sovereign nations. This distinction emphasizes the rules and systems that support tribal sovereignty, allowing tribes to have control over their own matters, including the care of their children. This helps ensure that tribes can make decisions that are best for their communities and cultures. But the US government has often challenged this special status, especially when it comes to land rights.

Regaining the Black Hills

The Lakota people consider the Black Hills, a mountain range extending between South Dakota and Wyoming, sacred and central to their culture. In 1868 the US government signed the Treaty of Fort Laramie, which guaranteed the Black Hills to the Lakota Nation. But in 1874 gold was discovered in the Black Hills. This led to an influx of settlers, miners, and the US military. The US government, eager to access the gold, violated the treaty and seized the Black Hills in 1877.

The Lakota, Dakota, and Nakota tribes (together known as the Sioux Nation) took several legal actions to regain the region. The most significant case was *United States v. Sioux Nation of Indians* in 1980. The Supreme Court ruled in favor of the Lakota, stating that the US government had unlawfully taken the Black Hills. The court awarded the tribe a $17.5 million financial settlement as compensation for the lost land. But the Lakota didn't want the payment—they wanted the land back. In 1985 and 1987 New Jersey senator Bill Bradley introduced legislation to Congress to help the Lakota regain their lost land, but opposition from legislators stopped the bill from moving forward.

In 2012 the UN conducted a twelve-day tour of Indigenous lands to determine if the US was following the UN Declaration of the Rights of Indigenous Peoples. The Declaration, adopted in 2007, serves as a global framework that sets standards for "the survival, dignity and well-being of the Indigenous peoples of the world." It outlines essential rights and protections that aim to ensure that Indigenous communities can thrive and maintain their cultures and identities. During the tour, the UN recommended returning some land to tribes, including the return of the Black Hills to the Lakota.

The Black Hills span 5,000 square miles (12,950 sq. km) of rugged rock formations, canyons, grasslands, streams, lakes, and caves. The name comes from the Lakota *Paha Sapa*, meaning "black hills," because their pine-covered slopes look black from a distance. Dakota elders also describe Paha Sapa as the "heart of all there is."

In 2016 the Department of the Interior and the BIA told the Oceti Sakowin (a group that includes Dakota, Lakota, and Nakota people) that they would put one of the sacred sites in the unreturned Black Hills into federal Indian trust status. Then in 2018, 1,020 acres (413 ha) of sacred land near Bear Butte in South Dakota was sold to the Northern Cheyenne Tribe of Montana and the Arapaho Tribe of Oklahoma in compliance with the UN's declaration. As of 2024 the Lakota are still demanding the full return of the Black Hills. But these other land sales highlight the ongoing efforts by all tribes to reclaim their sacred lands, fueling the Land Back movement, which focuses on restoring Indigenous control over ancestral territories.

Land Back Movement

The Land Back movement started in 2018. It helps people understand how tribal nations are working to reclaim the land taken from them. One of its main goals is to close Mount Rushmore, which is located in the Black Hills, and return all public lands in this area to Indigenous people.

More broadly, the campaign focuses on four demands. First, it seeks to dismantle the structures of white supremacy that forcefully removed Indigenous people from their lands and continue to oppress them. It also calls for the Bureau of Land Management and the National Parks Service to defund and stop supporting systems that uphold white supremacy and to reconnect Indigenous people with the stewardship of their lands. The movement also demands that other institutions such as the police, US Border Patrol, and Immigration and Customs Enforcement return all public lands to Indigenous people. Lastly, it advocates for Indigenous communities to be fully informed about potential projects or policies that affect their lands and to have the freedom to make their own governmental decisions.

REFLECT

How do you think returning land to Native nations could impact their communities now and into the future?

Increased Representation

While Indigenous communities are working to reclaim their ancestral lands, they are also pushing for stronger representation in government. By strengthening their voices in decision making, they aim to protect their rights, land, and communities. Although Native nations are independent and sovereign, federal decisions often affect them. And federal

Standing Rock Protests

Oil pipelines across North America often cross or come close to Indigenous lands, putting sacred sites, water sources, and cultural practices at risk. Tribal nations have long opposed these projects, which are frequently built without their consent. In 2016 Indigenous youth learned about a plan to build the Dakota Access Pipeline (DAPL) through sacred Dakota lands including the Standing Rock Reservation and under the Missouri River, threatening their water and cultural sites. The young leaders organized a cross-country run from North Dakota to Washington, DC. Their goal was to raise awareness and stop the pipeline.

They created the hashtag #NoDAPL, which quickly spread on platforms including Instagram, helping to raise awareness. Their message spread far beyond Standing Rock, bringing attention to the need to protect water, sacred lands, and Indigenous rights across North America. The peaceful protests brought together Indigenous tribes and non-Indigenous supporters, encouraging young people to fight for environmental and Indigenous causes for future generations.

The Oceti Sakowin protest camp near the Standing Rock Dakota Reservation became the central gathering place for those resisting DAPL. It brought together thousands of Indigenous people and their allies from around the world to protect water and sacred lands.

lawmakers don't often consider how their choices impact Native nations. Increased Indigenous representation in the federal government strengthens Native nations' voices.

Deb Haaland spoke at the White House Tribal Nations Summit in 2021. The summit brings together federal administrators and tribal leaders from the 574 federally recognized tribes to discuss ways the federal government can invest in and strengthen nation-to-nation relationships as well as ensure that progress in Indian Country endures for years to come.

Between 2021 and 2024, President Joe Biden nominated a historic number of Indigenous people to key federal positions. In 2021 Deb Haaland, a member of the Pueblo of Laguna, became the first Indigenous person to serve as a cabinet secretary. She focused on environmental justice, climate change, missing and murdered Indigenous women, Indian boarding school accountability, and removing offensive place names. Jaime Pinkham from the Nez Perce Tribe was appointed the principal deputy assistant secretary of the Army for Civil Works in 2021, and helped Indigenous communities manage water and land. In 2022 Marilynn Malerba, the lifetime chief of the Mohegan Tribe, became the US treasurer. She is the first Indigenous person whose signature appeared on US currency. As of 2025 five Indigenous members also serve in Congress, including Tom Cole, Sharice Davids, Mary Peltola, Josh Brecheen, and Markwayne Mullin.

CONCLUSION

Looking Forward

Indigenous people have lived in North America for thousands of generations, since long before recorded history. They have made significant contributions to land, law, and culture. Indigenous communities also play an essential role in protecting the environment, preserving their languages, and sharing knowledge with future generations. Respecting their sovereignty ensures that their voices are heard in decisions that affect them. Despite many challenges, they have remained strong, protecting traditions and fighting for their rights. Their work for self-determination, fair representation, and respect for their land is essential in working toward equality. Indigenous rights and sovereignty are not just issues for Indigenous people but are vital to society as a whole.

North American Indian Days is a culturally rich celebration held annually in Browning, Montana, on the Blackfeet Nation's reservation. It hosts tribes from every region of the US and Canada. The event features drumming and singing, which are integral to Indigenous cultural expression and spirituality.

Get Involved

Want to get involved in supporting Indigenous rights? Here's how you can!

- **Educate yourself and others.** Understanding Indigenous people's history, struggles, and contributions is the first step toward supporting their rights. To deepen your knowledge, engage with books, documentaries, podcasts, and Indigenous voices. Share what you learn with your friends, family, and others to build awareness in your community.
- **Support Indigenous-led movements and organizations.** Many Indigenous-led organizations are working to protect land rights, cultural heritage, and political autonomy. Supporting these organizations through donations, volunteering, or advocacy can amplify their efforts.
- **Advocate for policy changes.** Encourage your government representatives to support legislation strengthening Indigenous sovereignty, protecting their lands, and honoring treaties.
- **Honor treaties and agreements.** Ensure local and national governments honor existing treaties and agreements with Indigenous nations. This involves supporting efforts to uphold these legal commitments and opposing actions infringing on Indigenous rights.
- **Engage in collaborative efforts.** Foster partnerships with Indigenous communities by respecting their autonomy, seeking their input in matters that affect them, and advocating for them in spaces where their voices might not be heard.

By taking steps to support Indigenous rights and sovereignty, you can contribute to a future where Indigenous nations are acknowledged, empowered, and continue to thrive.

GLOSSARY

accountability: a willingness of individuals, organizations, or institutions to accept responsibility for their actions, decisions, and their consequences

activist: someone who actively campaigns for social or political change, often by participating in protests, demonstrations, or other forms of direct action

advocate: to publicly support or recommend a particular cause, policy, or idea

agency: a place set up by the US government to manage relations with Native nations and distribute resources promised in treaties. The Lower Sioux Agency was created to provide goods and oversee treaty obligations for the Dakota people in Minnesota.

allotment: a piece of land assigned to someone, often by the government

assimilate: to become part of a new culture or society, adopting its customs, traditions, or ways of life

autonomy: the ability to make one's own decisions rather than being directed by someone else

base rolls: official lists that the US government created in the 1800s to keep track of who belonged to different Indigenous tribes

census record: an official document that lists information about people living in a specific area such as their names, ages, and family relationships. The government uses this data to plan and provide services.

civilian: a person who is not on active duty in the armed forces or not on a police force

colonization: when a country establishes control over a group of people or area. A colony is a settlement that a country establishes outside of its territory.

constitution: a set of rules or guidelines that dictate how a government functions

convert: to change to a new religious belief

decree: an official order or decision issued by someone in government

discrimination: unjust treatment of people or groups of people based on certain characteristics, such as race or gender

exploitation: the act of treating someone or something unfairly for one's own benefit; to overuse resources without asking

federal recognition: a legal acknowledgment of the sovereign and separate political status of a tribal nation

imperial: related to an empire, where one powerful country controls or influences other lands, often through expansion and dominance over those areas.

legislation: a formal process of proposing, debating, and passing laws that govern how people behave and interact in society

oppress: to treat someone or a group of people unfairly, often by using power or authority to control or limit their rights, freedom, or opportunities

reservation: a piece of land set aside by the US government for Indigenous tribes to live on and govern themselves

reserve: a tract of land set aside under the Indian Act in Canada for the exclusive use of a tribal nation

segregation: the enforced separation of individuals or groups based on certain characteristics such as race, ethnicity, religion, or gender

social worker: a person who is trained to help individuals, families, and communities cope with various challenges

stewardship: traditional and contemporary practices of caring for and managing the natural environment that ensures its sustainability for future generations

suffrage: the right to vote

systemic injustice: the unfair treatment that is built into the rules, laws, and institutions of a society. This type of injustice affects groups of people over time and makes it difficult for them to access the same opportunities and rights as others.

trauma: a term used to describe deeply distressing or harmful experiences that can have lasting effects on a person's mental or emotional well-being

treaty: a legal contract between nations

tribal trust status: a legal arrangement where the US government holds and manages land for Indigenous tribes to protect it from being sold, taken, or developed without a tribe's consent

tribe: a social group comprised of families or clans of different generations having a shared ancestry and language

white supremacy: the false belief that the white race is superior to other races and that white people should have more power and control over people of other races. The term also refers to the social, economic, and political systems that allow white people to keep that power.

SOURCE NOTES

7 "With fifty men . . . of these slaves.": "Journal of the First Voyage of Columbus," Wisconsin Historical Society Digital Library and Archives, 2003, https://www.americanjourneys.org/AJ_PDF/AJ-062.pdf.

8 "the church acknowledges . . . of Indigenous peoples.": Nicole Winfield, "Vatican Formally Denounces 15th-Century 'Doctrine of Discovery,' Used to Justify Colonizing Indigenous Peoples," *America Magazine*, March 30, 2023, https://www.americamagazine.org/faith/2023/03/30/indigenous-vatican-catholic-church-discovery-doctrine-americas-244997.

23 "We have waited . . . ourselves from starving.": "Causes of the War, US Dakota War," Minnesota Historical Society, accessed September 18, 2024, https://www.usdakotawar.org/history/war/causes-war.

23 "If they are . . . their own dung.": "Andrew Myrick, US Dakota War," Minnesota Historical Society, accessed September 18, 2024, https://www.usdakotawar.org/history/andrew-myrick.

24 "We are only . . . you can count.": "Little Crow's Speech," Minnesota Libraries Publishing Project, accessed September 24, 2024, https://mlpp.pressbooks.pub/woundedknee/chapter/primary-sources/.

29 "I do not . . . add to it.": Abi Fain, Mary Kathryn Nagle, "Close to Zero: The Reliance on Minimum Blood Quantum Requirements to Eliminate Tribal Citizenship in the Allotment Acts and the Post-Adoptive Couple Challenges to the Constitutionality of ICWA," *Mitchell Hamline Law Review*, Vol 43, Issue 4, Article 4.

40 "If a one-day . . . to the island.": Evan Andrews, "When Native American Activists Occupied Alcatraz Island," History.com, April 25, 2024, https://www.history.com/news/native-american-activists-occupy-alcatraz-island-45-years-ago.

49 "the survival, dignity . . . of the world": "UN Declaration on the Rights of Indigenous Peoples," Australian Human Rights Commission, accessed October 30, 2024, https://humanrights.gov.au/our-work/un-declaration-rights-indigenous-people.

SELECTED BIBLIOGRAPHY

Blackhawk, Ned. *The Rediscovery of America: Native Peoples and the Unmaking of US History*. New Haven, CT: Yale University Press, 2023.

DeLucia, Christine, et al. "Histories of Indigenous Sovereignty in Action: What Is It and Why Does It Matter?" Organization of American Historians. Accessed November 22, 2024. https://www.oah.org/tah/native-american-history-and-sovereignty/histories-of-indigenous-sovereignty-in-action-what-is-it-and-why-does-it-matter/.

Dunbar-Ortiz, Roxanne. *An Indigenous Peoples' History of the United States*. Boston: Beacon Press, 2015.

Sleeper-Smith, Susan, Juliana Barr, Jean M. O'Brien, Nancy Shoemaker, and Scott Manning Stevens. *Why You Can't Teach United States History Without American Indians*. Chapel Hill, NC: University of North Carolina Press, 2015.

Treuer, David. *The Heartbeat of Wounded Knee: Native America from 1890 to Present*. New York: Riverhead Books, 2019.

"US Indian Boarding School History." The National Native American Boarding School Healing Coalition. Accessed November 22, 2024. https://boardingschoolhealing.org/education/us-indian-boarding-school-history/.

Zinn, Howard. *A People's History of the United States*. New York: Harper Perennial Modern Classics, 2015.

FURTHER INFORMATION

Books

Kimmerer, Robin Wall, and Monique Gray Smith. *Braiding Sweetgrass for Young Adults: Indigenous Wisdom, Scientific Wisdom, and the Teachings of Plants*. Minneapolis: Zest Books, 2022.
Adapted from the adult version, this book is full of Indigenous wisdom and explains Indigenous people's role in the world, how to understand the land, and how to be stewards of the land. Explore the interconnectedness of all living things. Learn about the healing power of plants, the importance of gratitude, and Indigenous ways to care for the environment.

Smith, Nareissa. *Fighting for Equality: Racial Justice in North America*. Minneapolis: Twenty-First Century Books, 2025.
With a focus on reflection, this book not only educates readers about the historical and contemporary challenges faced by marginalized groups in North America but also empowers readers to become agents of change in the ongoing fight for justice.

Treuer, Anton. *Everything You Wanted to Know about Indians but Were Afraid to Ask: Young Readers Edition*. Hoboken, NJ: Levin Querido, 2021.
This collection of essays answers dozens of questions exploring racism, identity, traditions, and more. It also includes a social activism section.

Treuer, David, and Shelia Keenan. *The Heartbeat of Wounded Knee (Young Readers Adaptation): Life in Native America*. New York: Viking, 2022.
Adapted from the adult version, this book lays out Indigenous history from 1890 until modern times. It explores the resilience and ongoing stories of Indigenous life, focusing on the period after the infamous Wounded Knee Massacre of 1890.

Webstad, Phyllis. *Beyond the Orange Shirt Story*. Victoria, British Columbia: Medicine Wheel Publishing, 2021.
This book brings together personal stories from survivors of residential schools and their families, sharing experiences before, during, and after their time in the schools. This collection offers readers a firsthand perspective on the impact of these schools on Indigenous lives and families, conveyed through the authentic voices of those who lived it.

Websites

American Indian Movement

https://www.aimovement.org/

This website gives insight into the history and current efforts of the American Indian Movement. It is a great resource for understanding the fight for civil rights and sovereignty.

Indigenous Environmental Network

https://www.ienearth.org/

This website highlights the intersection of Indigenous rights and environmental activism. Learn about Indigenous land protection, climate justice, and movements that focus on both Indigenous cultural heritage and the planet.

National Congress of American Indians

https://www.ncai.org/

This organization provides a wealth of information about current Indigenous rights, policies, and advocacy. Learn about key legal battles, ongoing activism, and important policy decisions affecting Indigenous communities.

National Museum of the American Indian

https://americanindian.si.edu/online-resources

Explore topics including Indigenous culture and identity, boarding schools, social justice, and history. Look at thousands of objects online that reflect the historical and contemporary lives of Indigenous peoples. Part of the Smithsonian Institution, this website also hosts online exhibits, a magazine, and activities focusing on Indigenous lives.

United Nations: International Day of the World's Indigenous Peoples

https://www.un.org/en/observances/indigenous-day

This page highlights Indigenous peoples globally, their contributions, and the challenges they face. Explore various topics related to Indigenous rights, the environment, and social justice on an international scale.

INDEX

ABOUT THE AUTHOR

Heather Bruegl is a citizen of the Oneida Nation of Wisconsin who lives in Detroit, Michigan. She works as a curator, lecturer, and public historian. Her areas of expertise include early colonial, revolutionary, presidential, and Indigenous history. When not writing or lecturing, she enjoys traveling, baking, reading, and a good cup of hot chocolate.

PHOTO ACKNOWLEDGMENTS

The images in this book are used with the permission of: © Dimitrios Karamitros/iStockphoto, p. 7; © duncan1890/iStockphoto, p. 9; © Library of Congress, pp. 11, 13; © Glasshouse Images/Alamy Photo, p. 17; © The Picture Art Collection/Alamy Photo, p. 19; © Wikimedia Commons, pp. 21, 27; © Percy Jackson II/AP Images, p. 22; © Library of Congress, p. 24; © Classic Image/Alamy Photo, p. 25; © Library of Congress/Wikimedia Commons, p. 32; © Nick Nickels/Government of Canada, p. 33; © U.S. National Archives and Records, p. 35; © Danita Delimont/Alamy Photo, p. 37; © Tribune Content Agency LLC/Alamy Photo, p. 38; © Kalle Benallie/AP Images, p. 39; © Anonymous/AP Images, p. 40; © Everett Collection Inc/Alamy Photo, p. 43; © Henry Burroughs/AP Images, p. 44; © ZUMA Press, Inc./Alamy Photo, p. 48; © Jim Parkin/Shutterstock Images, p. 50; © AlexanderGouletas/iStockphoto, p. 52; © MediaPunch Inc/Alamy Photo, p. 53; © John Reddy/Alamy Photo, p. 54.

Cover Photo: © RichVintage/iStockphoto

Design Elements: © Ezhevika/Shutterstock Images